I READ! YOU READ!

 Child's Turn to Read    Adult's Turn to Read

WE READ ABOUT Maevis USING HER MANNERS

Written by
Vicky Bureau
M.S., School Counseling
and
Madison Parker

Illustrated by
Flavia Zuncheddu

SEAHORSE PUBLISHING

Parent and Caregiver Guide

Reading aloud with your child has many benefits. It expands vocabulary, sparks discussion, and promotes an emotional bond. Research shows that children who have books read aloud to them have improved language skills, leading to greater school success.

I Read! You Read! books offer a fun and easy way to read with your child. Follow these guidelines.

Before Reading

- Look at the front and back covers. Discuss personal experiences that relate to the topic.
- Read the *Words to Know* at the back of the book. Talk about what the words mean.
- If the book will be challenging or unfamiliar to your child, read it aloud by yourself the first time. Then, invite your child to participate in a second reading.

During Reading

 Have your child read the words beside this symbol. This text has been carefully matched to the reading and grade levels shown on the cover.

 You read the words beside this symbol.

- Stop often to discuss what you are reading and to make sure your child understands.
- If your child struggles with decoding a word, help them sound it out. If it is still a challenge, say the word for your child and have them repeat it after you.
- To find the meaning of a word, look for clues in the surrounding words and pictures.

After Reading

- Praise your child's efforts. Notice how they have grown as a reader.
- Use the *Comprehension Questions* at the back of the book.
- Discuss what your child learned and what they liked or didn't like about the book.

Most importantly, let your child know that reading is fun and worthwhile. Keep reading together as your child's skills and confidence grow.

TABLE OF CONTENTS

Meet Maevis 4

What Are Manners? 6

Using Good Manners 8

Words to Know 22

Index 23

Comprehension Questions 23

Meet Maevis

This is Maevis.

School **manners** matter to Maevis.

School **manners** are the rules and **expectations** for learning.

What Are Manners?

Manners are behaviors that show others kindness, respect, and **courtesy**.

Maevis uses her manners to be **mindful** of others.

Using Good Manners

Maevis sits with a friend who is alone at lunch.

Maevis is kind.

Maevis says "please" and "thank you."

Maevis is **respectful**.

Maevis holds the door for her teacher.

Maevis raises her hand before speaking.

Maevis uses her manners in the classroom.

Maevis shares her pretzels at snack time.

Maevis uses her manners in the cafeteria.

Maevis uses her manners on the playground.

Maevis is **mindful** about how she makes others feel.

That's why Maevis minds her manners!

WORDS TO KNOW

courtesy (KUR-ti-see): good manners or politeness

expectations (ek-spek-TAY-shuhnz): the rules that tell us what is okay to do and not to do

manners (MAN-urs): the rules and expectations for learning; good behaviors

mindful (MINDE-fuhl): being careful and paying close attention

respectful (ri-SPEKT-fuhl): showing that you admire and pay attention to someone or something

INDEX

cafeteria 17
classroom 15
kind(ness) 6, 9

playground 19
respect(ful) 6, 10
shares 16, 18

COMPREHENSION QUESTIONS

1. What are manners?
2. Based on the story, name one way you can be kind to others.
3. What does Maevis share on the playground?
4. Who does Maevis sit with at lunch?

Written by: Vicky Bureau and Madison Parker
Illustrated by: Flavia Zuncheddu
Design by: Under the Oaks Media
Editor: Kim Thompson

Library of Congress PCN Data
We Read About Maevis Using Her Manners / Vicky Bureau and Madison Parker
I Read! You Read!
ISBN 979-8-8873-5306-7 (hard cover)
ISBN 979-8-8873-5391-3 (paperback)
ISBN 979-8-8873-5476-7 (EPUB)
ISBN 979-8-8873-5561-0 (eBook)
Library of Congress Control Number: 2022951082

Printed in the United States of America.

Seahorse Publishing Company
www.seahorsepub.com

Copyright © 2024 **SEAHORSE PUBLISHING COMPANY**

All rights reserved. No part of this publication may be reproduced, stored in a retrieval system or be transmitted in any form or by any means, electronic, mechanical, photocopying, recording, or otherwise, without the prior written permission of Seahorse Publishing Company.

Published in the United States
Seahorse Publishing
PO Box 771325
Coral Springs, FL 33077